# *BLOG POWER AND SOCIAL MEDIA HANDBOOK*

## *A Cultural E-volution*

How to become a
successful blogger and
find your place in the
social networking
scene

**Helen Gallagher**

*Author: Release Your Writing: Book Publishing Your Way*

Ver. 2

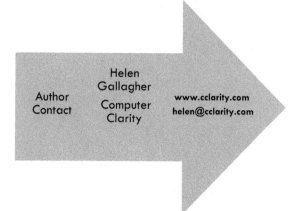

Author Contact

Helen Gallagher

Computer Clarity

www.cclarity.com
helen@cclarity.com

# Contents

## Blog Power and Social Media Handbook

# Contents - continued

*Blog Power and Social Media Handbook*
helps you find your place in Web 2.0 culture

About the book:

*Blog Power and Social Media Handbook* provides an overview of how Web 2.0 came about and how its changed since it first popped up in 2004. Also called social networking, Web 2.0 is a new phase of the internet: reaching out to web users for a shared experience, rather than delivery of static web pages or the one-way commentary on most sites. Broadly defined, Web 2.0 is the interactive version of the web, with blogs and social media sites, such as Facebook and Twitter dominating society's communication and news stream today.

Corporations are in billion-dollar bidding wars to claim ownership of these online services, because the users represent massive potential revenue for advertisers.

But what do these sites do? Who has time to use them, and what effect will they have on literacy and culture? This is a worldwide issue that has a significant effect on what children are doing in school, how they learn, and what they will become.

The old "information superhighway" was a one-way street. If we wanted information, we went to a web site and retrieved it. Today it's all about a collaborative, interactive social networking experience, for better or worse.

*Blog Power and Social Media Handbook* was published both in print and in ebook format specifically so the ebook can be updated as the fast-paced web world changes. Bulk purchase information for both versions is available at the author's web site, Computer Clarity, www.cclarity.com. Special pricing is available for schools and libraries worldwide.

*Helen Gallagher*

**Author contact: Helen@cclarity.com**
**© 2010, Helen Gallagher**

# Where it began...

New things come about because there's room for them in society, because what we already have isn't perfect, and because there's big money to be made. Hence Web 2.0, the second generation of the Internet, where static web pages are replaced by interactive sites, with content contributed by users and shared instantly with the public.

This social networking or social media is the new face of the internet: reaching out to web users for a shared experience, rather than delivery of static web pages or the one-way commentary on most blogs.

Things change fast in technology. MySpace used to have 80 percent of the social networking market. Then thousands of MySpace users jumped over to Facebook, and tomorrow may hop over to the next new thing. What will it be? Maybe Twiddle, Doofus, or another time-drain...or whatever else the venture capitalists can create. As of this writing, Hi5.com has come along, the newest kid on the block for fun and self-expression.

The story doesn't end there. We consider the effect these social sites have on creating buzz for a hit book, movie or celebrity-chasing. The power of Twitter and Facebook to sway public opinion is startling. The instant nature of this new form of communication has inherent problems, including concern over the move away from trained journalists to consumers creating their own news, unfiltered.

# THE MYSTERIOUS WORLD
# OF WEB 2.0

First there was the **Internet** in the 1960s.

Then, with the invention of hypertext, the **worldwide web** became a graphical interface for internet content in 1991.

**Web 2.0** is the umbrella term for all that has come since then... Using the web not in a static way to deliver web content, but as an integrated, participatory way to socialize, involve and engage viewers, contributing web content we hope is worth the reader's time and attention.

**Social media** is where we are now, using the organized aggregation and delivery of integrated text, audio, and video. The social element comes about because people started to email each other interesting links, then services like Facebook got people to sign up, have a page to post what they like, and draw others to the site, with exponential growth unseen in human history.

**Acronym Madness:** A new shorthand, used by people typing on thumb pads and cell phones. Very common now as abbreviations and typing quick Twitter messages, which are limited to 140 characters.

AFAIK As far as I know
BBL Be back later
B4N Bye for now
BRB Be right back
BTW By the way
CUL8R See you later
F2F Face-to-face
FWIW For what it's worth
GOI Get over it
IMHO In my humble opinion
IOH I'm outta here
IOW In other words
IRL In real life
ITS I told you so
KIT Keep in touch
LOL Laughing out loud
LTL Lets talk later
LTNS Long time no see

NM Nothing much
NOYB None of your business
NP No problem
NRN No reply needed
OHM Oh my God
OTP On the phone
PMFJI Pardon me for jumping in
POS Parents over shoulder
POV Point of view
ROTFL Rolling on the floor laughing
RUOK Are you okay?
TIA Thanks in advance
TMI or 2MI Too much information
TTFN Ta Ta for now
TTYL Talk to you later
UKW You know who

You'll find a huge acronym list at:
www.netlingo.com/emailsh.cfm

# Part One

# Blog Power

Fundamentals

Where and how to start

The power of blogs

The blogger community

# Blog Power

The fundamentals:

Where do blogs fit in the social media category?

Blogs aren't quite social media because they don't exist just to create dialog and chat with others. They are also becoming credible sources for news and opinion.

Blogs are a web-based platform to post information. Some have a broad scope where the writer discusses whatever is on his or her mind, others focus on a narrow topic, such as cooking, illness and recovery, quilting, personal essays, job hunting, travel, literature, or any other areas of interest.

A blog is like a web site, but it displays a writer's posts in chronological order, and is searchable by category of the topics. Comments are invited, links to other blogs or sites are often shared, widening the resources for the reader. Sidebars are optional, directing readers to other interesting items.

**TIP: There is a generous section at the back of the book for you to write notes as you go along.**

"If you are writing the clearest, truest words you can find and doing the best you can to understand and communicate, this will shine on paper like its own little lighthouse. Lighthouses don't go running all over an island looking for boats to save; they just stand there shining."

--Anne Lamott

author: *Bird By Bird,*

*Some Instructions on Writing and Life*

Of all the power tools in today's web world, a blog may
be the most versatile. Consider a blog as a way to
gain exposure for your other work, whether it is raising
children, running a non-profit, or a dog-washing
service. It's great exposure, and an outlet for you to
post your ideas and stimulate discussions.

Wondering why blogs are chronological? It's based on
their origin as web diaries (web-log). When you visit a
blog the newest information is usually posted at the top
for quick access. You can get around the chronological
layout, if it doesn't suit your purpose, by using links to
organize the content. A blog is not a perfect
replacement for the depth that a website offers. It's a
nice counterpoint, though, easy to update, always fresh
and topical.

# Where and how to start

Perhaps the best way to pull yourself into blog culture is to start one. Free blogs are available through Blogger.com (owned by Google), LiveJournal.com and WordPress.com. Typepad blogs start at $8.95/month.

Name your blog. If you choose a name such as "A Nose for Wine," that's how people will find your blog. At Blogger.com it would be anoseforwine.blogspot.com and at Wordpress it would be anoseforwine.wordpress.com.
(Note: all lowercase, no punctuation except dash or dot.)

You can purchase a domain name for less than $20/year, so you can use your own dot-com, such as timscollegeblog.com, instead of showing the blog host name.

Once you sign up, choose a design template, and create your first blog post. Then return to it when your muse beckons. Blog posts are generally short, contain links of interest, and invite comments. Styles are far from conventional, so anything goes.

The first thing you'll notice about blog writing is that it's different than other writing. There is an obvious shift from the five W's of journalism to a quicker pace and rhythm. A unique voice and personal style is what captures and keeps reader attention. Shorter paragraphs work best. Break up text with images and vary your pace.

Here's are typical guidelines:

- **Titles** - A catchy title will get noticed. Be clever or factual but don't go too far.

- **Structure** - Like an essay, a blog entry should have a topic sentence and a focus. Early on, the reader should discern why they are reading and see the relevance of the title.

- **Uniformity** - The more professional you want your blog to be, the more cohesive the topics should be. Have more than one blog if you want a space to rant about laundry, sex and groceries. Keep the professional blog focused on topics germane to your primary focus., so readers will return.

There are other mechanical aspects of blog management you can learn over time. Starting out, you'll want to know how to make a new post, insert images and links, and use Labels or Tags, to categorize your post.

As shown on the following page, labels and tags are powerful tools to sort all your posts by topic.

Other tools you'll enjoy exploring are referred to as gadgets and widgets, such as:

- Slideshows and video clips
- A 'hit counter' showing how many people visit your blog,
- A search box for people to find specific keywords,
- A "blog roll' to display links to other blogs you like,
- Links to purchase related books from online booksellers, and Google ads if you want to earn money when people click an ad on your blog.
- Your blog photo can be any image, your photo, a pet, an object, usually called an Avatar or Gravatar.

Blog labels, tags and clouds:

The labels or tags in a blog provide a great way to organize related posts, so if someone enjoys your comments on "visibility," and they click the visibility link shown in a format like this, they'll see any other posts on that topic. The size in which the font is displayed signifies the number of blog posts on that topic. Clever, isn't it?

Sample tag cloud from my blog for authors at
pajamamarketing.wordpress.com.

## Blog writing

Whether you're new to writing or a pro, it helps to understand the distinction between opinion writing and reporting. Most blogs convey the author's opinion on topical matters. If you blog professionally, you'll want to provide useful information, but be careful not to give too much information away for free. For example, if you're a life coach, leave the person wanting to know more, and direct them to your web site or your books for more specific information.

As with all writing, you own the copyright to your work the moment you write it, but use careful judgment in taking information from other sources for use on your own blog. Always cite your sources, and provide a link back to the source for more details.

CreativeCommons.org allows content creators to legally share free content online, while retaining copyright. If your blog includes terrific original photos you might also distribute them via Creative Commons, to protect your copyright.

Blog writing styles vary, but the best way to start out is writing short and swift, with clarity and focus. It's good to keep posts brief, perhaps 400 words, since people are a) reading on the screen, and b) likely to get distracted when the eye wanders off to the sidebars on your blog, and not finish reading.

Blogs can be set to allow or prohibit comments from readers. Most blogs get few comments, and they're not always favorable. Don't pay any attention to negative comments, and its best to reply only to specific requests for information. Your blog can be configured to require your approval before comments are posted. Delete the spam and inappropriate comments, and forget about them.

As Will Rogers said:

"Don't let yesterday use up too much of today."

# Blog Communities

The best place to begin, if you're really new to blogs, is to start on the receiving end.

Take a look at blogs in your area of interest. Note how often they are updated, what you like and dislike, and whether they have ads. Do the blog posts link to longer articles and to other resources? Do you like blogs that use a relevant image to accompany each post? Do other bloggers ask readers to leave comments? Do the sidebars distract you?

On a sheet of paper, as you're viewing various blogs, create an "I Can Do This..." idea list. Or... download the idea list you see on the following page. It's free at cclarity.com/blogbookcando.doc.

# I CAN DO THIS....

**BLOG NAME IDEAS**

| | |
|---|---|
| | |
| | |
| | |
| | |

**PHOTOS**

| | |
|---|---|
| | |
| | |
| | |
| | |

**START AN EMAIL LIST**

| | |
|---|---|
| | |
| | |
| | |
| | |

**SCHEDULE**

| | | |
|---|---|---|
| | DATE: | BLOG POST 1 |
| | DATE: | BLOG POST 2 |
| | DATE: | BLOG POST 3 |
| | DATE: | BLOG POST 4 |

**FUTURE IDEAS**

| | |
|---|---|
| | |
| | |
| | |

Okay, are you ready to blog?

Take a look at Blogger.com and Wordpress.com. Blogger is the easiest blog tool to use but Wordpress has more gadgets and cool tools. Both offer free templates, and a simple sign-up process.

Some color schemes seem appropriate for specific blog topics — calm colors for a compassionate feel, bold primary colors for high energy blogs. Notice which ones you respond to, and what would work with your blog's theme. Have fun with it.

Start from where you are; you can always improve or change your blog over time.

Blogging essential: **Know your goals**

For your blog, or any writing, your "voice" is the most important element. Would you read a whiny, screechy, crabby blog, or the thoughts of a sincere, informed person with a focused message?

Your specific blog goals will require some thought, but in general you might aim to:

- Increase visitors to your web site
- Make new connections
- Have people purchase products/services

Be honest in assessing whether you seek fame and fortune or whether you'll be happy just being heard; a voice in the wilderness, reaching people interested in reading what you have to say.

Don't underestimate the power of your blog to make a difference, and to engage people in conversation. Keep your voice consistent with your beliefs and your goals, but also consider engaging with readers and adapting your content based on their feedback.

Once you get proficient at blogging, and earn the trust of your readers, take your social media efforts a step further. Use your readers as a springboard for further ideas, suggestions for volunteering, meeting places and agendas. Or ask them for feedback on what else they need to hear from you. Why? The more you give them what they want, the more they will return, bring friends, and grow your readership.

Remember your top reasons for that growing audience:

1. Potential to spin the topic into a book
2. Show credibility to get hired for a job, non-profit, campaign manager, or as a paid blogger

The more you understand your reader, the more potential exposure for you.

As your blog grows over time, it becomes the core of your online presence. When you communicate with people on social media sites, such as Facebook, Twitter and LinkedIn, they will visit your blog to learn more about what you do. Since a blog is free, with no recurring hosting fees or cumbersome web site updates, a blog is the perfect vehicle for you to have a fresh, sharp, polished profile online.

Remember though, if you don't know what you want to say, its quite likely no one will want to read it.

You may find, because you have the blog as an outlet, you will likely get more ideas about what to write, and be more creative because you have a place to post your thoughts and ideas, and share information

As a blogger, you might even let a few great people into your world; people you wouldn't likely meet otherwise. There are so many fascinating blogs, that you'll soon find yourself linking to others and perhaps even getting hired to write for a blog. So enjoy the experience. It provides a great introduction to the rest of the Web 2.0 world, with social media sites, which is covered in Part Two.

## Technical note:

RSS (really-simple syndication) lets you receive newsfeed from Google, Yahoo (shown below) and other sources, so you will know when your blog or topic is mentioned elsewhere online. It's easy to get started...

# Anatomy of a blog post

Similar to an email format, the **Title** is like an email subject
line, and the **Body** is your message. There are icons to
help you insert images and create links. The **Labels** box
below the post is where you put in the words that will
sort your posts by topic.

Blogger.com screenshot:

As you get more comfortable with blog writing, and as you read other good blogs, you'll learn to vary the content of your posts. Offer something of value – don't waste time with a good post title that doesn't live up to the hype.

Take the time to spice up the format – font size, color, and include images for visual appeal.

The best blogs, from zenhabits to lifehacker are image heavy and appealing because of the visual indication of the exciting stories behind them.

Some ideas to vary your content include:

Q & A format

Invite guest posts

Link directly to articles or videos you find elsewhere

Lists... people love lists

Opinion essays

Alter the length: While 300 words might be right for some posts, there's nothing wrong with a brief, thoughtful post

Contests (be careful: State regulations vary for contests).

A note on images and graphics

While graphics spice up the look of your blog, don't use images that belong to others.

Search for free web graphics or use high quality graphics from my favorite resource: morguefile.com, or other royalty-free graphic sites.

# Search engines and directories

Blogs are one of the best way to be found online. Because the content changes frequently, when web crawlers and search engines scan the web, your blog will likely show up well in searches. This is especially true of Blogger.com because its owned by Google.

For your blog to rank high in the search engines, it does need frequent, fresh content, and tags/labels that help categorize the content. In addition, blogs with a high number of inbound links score well.

> Inbound links are when other sites or blogs have a link back to yours. An outbound link is when you have a link on your blog, back to mine. That benefits me more than you, so inbound links are what you would strive for if search visibility is important to you.

Getting your blog listed in search engines and blog directories takes some time, but is pretty simple. Start with technorati.com, and do a web search for "blog directories" to find free opportunities to get linked. Blogcatalog.com will help you find blogs related to your category.

# SEO

Search engine optimization (SEO) is a lucrative field for developers and a large marketing expense for companies who want maximum visibility online.

The way to get noticed online is to show up high in search engine rankings. The term "search engine optimization" (SEO) refers to the use of keywords, and repetition to be found easily. That drives more traffic to your blog or site, and helps you connect with readers. SEO is big business, tracking click-thru rates and repeated visits to your blog.

TIP: You can also set a Google Alert so if your name or your blog's name shows up anywhere online, you'll get notified via email. People who have an alert set for your topic, such as 'adoption' or 'sustainable gardening' will see your blog in search results, and be directed to you.

There is no particular trick to writing SEO-friendly blog posts and you don't need any special skill or software.

1. Good blog writing will give good SEO results. Use good descriptive words that will attract people interested in your topic.

2. Use good titles: That's why the name of your blog is so important — as is the name of particular post titles. You want titles to look compelling when people come across them in search results or in a blog list. Those inbound referrals from other blogs carry more weight, because of the exponential expansion of the links from multiple sites that link to each other.

3. Tune up your writing and make sure you use context-specific words in your posts for good visibility online. You have to read other blogs and do a few web searches within your topic to learn what keywords relate well to your topic.

Your social networking sites lead back to your blog as the core

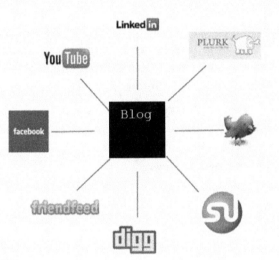

ProBlogger.net

With this foundation, are you ready to start blogging? I don't actually believe blogging can be taught. After reading this Blog Power background information, I hope its something you'll explore. Sign up, create a name, choose a template, and begin to blog.

As for what to blog about, I'm sure you'll be full of ideas after you explore other blogs. The content has to come from you – based on your areas of interest and your unique point of view.

# Blog Power Summary

Of all the power tools in today's web world, blogs may be the most versatile.

Good blog software is available for free. Blogs are easy to work with, and give you a place to explore and share your ideas.

As we've shown, a blog can become the foundation of your online platform. Your social media profiles can all link back to your blog.

If someone searches your name at Google, your blog will show up.

If you want to write for other blogs, or write magazine articles, your blog will showcase your writing style.

If you have strong ideas and beliefs on any topic, your blog is a vehicle for you to organize and convey your thoughts to the world.

Like many people, you may end up with a blog that's worth turning into a book. Search "blog to book" and you'll find all the resources needed to publish your blog.

# Part Two

# Social Media

Where it began

What it does

History

Effects on society

Benefits

The big three services

Web 2.0 provides a place where anyone can create a public profile and build a personal network to connect to like-minded online users. Web 2.0 sites include MySpace, Facebook, and Flickr (which had 3,842 photos uploaded in the last minute, as I write this). Typical content on social media sites might be text, chat, video, and personalized pages to track friends, events, and interests.

But what do these sites do? Who has time to use them, and what effect will they have on literacy and culture? This is a worldwide issue that has significant effect on what children are doing in school, how they learn, and what they will become.

Today, web use is all about a collaborative, interactive social networking experience, for better or worse.

According to Pew Internet & American Life Project:

**46%** of online American adults 18 and older use a social networking site like MySpace, Facebook or LinkedIn, up from 8% in February 2005.

**65%** of teens 12-17 use online social networks as of Feb 2008, up from 58% in 2007 and 55% in 2006.

http://www.pewinternet.org/Infographics/Growth-in-Adult-SNS-Use-20052009.aspx

Web 2.0 is more of an attitude than technology. Newspapers also presume an inner awareness of vernacular, language and meaning. Arriving here from another country, would you understand this newspaper headline? "Big 3, UAW at critical juncture." Is it referring to airplanes, sports teams? That's strange language for automakers and a union, but it creeps into common usage and becomes the norm.

So today we talk of blogs, YouTube, Wiki's, Facebook and tweets, all of which open doors for people to share and collaborate. Early sites developed for photo and music sharing proved millions of people would use these online portals, and today it has spread to people sharing comments, opinions, photos, friends, and poking each other all day on sites like Twitter.com where you tell friends what are you doing.

As fortunes are made, and investors reap profits, it's likely Web 2.0 and its social media sites will form the basis for a new kind of online life, blending reality and fantasy, truth and nonsense, leaving it to the web user to discern the value.

To avoid wasting time or straying too far, learn to recognize sites with contributed content and sites that aggregate popular information. Stick with those that place restrictions on input, rather than a web community. Those ad-hoc sites are poorly written and may be filled with personal opinion, not necessarily based in fact.

And who knows, maybe some day instead of draining our focus and productivity, these sites will benefit society, providing better communication services for those with disabilities, creating more efficient processes for home-based workers, or even making people smarter.

Could they one day represent the world's largest fact-filled database? Or could they vanish? We'll see...

Until then, we're watching people use massive internet resources to display videos of a bicycling dog, baby hippos, and an unending stream of drunken karaoke singers. Let's find out why . . .

# Social Networking Usage Statistics:

from Pew Internet & American Life Project

- 89 percent of adults surveyed use their online profile to keep up with friends

- 57 percent use their profile to make plans with friends

- 49 percent use them to make new friends

- 51 percent of social network users have two or more online profiles

- 43 percent have only one online profile

- Over 53 million Americans used the internet to publish their thoughts, post pictures, share files, etc.

- 85 percent have ever used search engines

- Only sending and reading email outranks search engine queries as an online activity.

Pew data gathered in national phone survey (November 19 to December 20, 2008 among 2,253 Americans, including 1,650 internet users. Margin of error=+/- 3%

http://www.pewinternet.org/Reports/2009/Adults-and-Social-Network-Websites.aspx?r=1

# The history...

Web 2.0 has become more pervasive than most of the experts thoughts. A few years ago, more teens than adults embraced this technology. Now things are different:

The internet takes on a different shape today. New ideas catch on because there's room for them... and because what we have already isn't perfect.... and because there's money to be made.

Hence Web 2.0, the second generation :

A place where a web user can create a public profile and build a personal network to connect to like-minded online users. So use of Web 2.0 is more of an attitude than technology.

This all seems successful and fun, so what's the problem? It is nearly inescapable today, but will it be gone tomorrow? Is social networking worth your time?

Explore the many ways successful entrepreneurs are working with social media sites such as Facebook, Twitter, and LinkedIn, to sustain their visibility and add credibility. As part of a professional platform, these avenues can open doors, put your work in front of the right people, and keep you connected with the larger world.

When Tim Berners-Lee first invented the graphical interface for the web in 1991, he designed it as a device to allow people to work together, using hypertext documents to combine information from different sources. Little did he know what that shared ability would become today.

You'll find fascinating information on Tim Berners-Lee here:
http://www.w3.org/People/Berners-Lee/FAQ.html

In late 2007, at Michigan State University, Jane Briggs-Bunting, director of the school of journalism, was in the news for sharing her views of this virtual world. She states:

"The freshmen enrolling at our colleges and universities today have grown up surrounded by technology— and it's just a tool to them... Many have created their own identities in virtual worlds like Second Life, where no one knows if they are 12 or 45... They are impatient, energetic, live on their cells and text their friends constantly. Frankly, most of them don't get what we do. They are news consumers, but have no brand loyalty."

The Guardian, U.K. newspaper quotes Richard Sambrook, the director of the BBC Global News Division, in September, 2009 ...

- "There is a transformation for the journalist from being the gatekeeper of information to sharing it in a public space. Therefore citizen journalism is something, Sambrook added, that has to be taken into account. However, he doesn't see the internet as a place where news come from — although Sky News has a Twitter correspondent researching the micro-blogging platform.

- Information is not journalism, he explained further. You get a lot of things, when you open up Twitter in the morning, but not journalism. Journalism needs discipline, analysis, explanation and context, he pointed out, and therefore for him it is still a profession. The value that gets added with journalism is judgment, analysis and explanation - and that makes the difference.

# So, maybe you're asking…

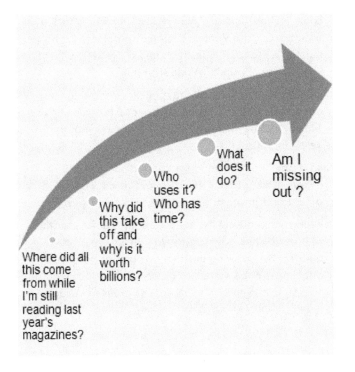

# Remember where we started?

When we first used the internet, everything was amazing: Look! There's *Time* and *Newsweek* and then, Martha Stewart. Oh, the Vatican is on the web! Here's a MOMA exhibit, a French film festival, and a live web-cam of the River Liffey in Dublin. Wonderful stuff!

Now, Web 2.0 has spun all that one-sided viewing into participatory sites built around peer interaction. In fact, *Time Magazine* named Web 2.0 the "Person of the Year" in 2006.

When bigger better computers came along, the differentiating factor they brought along was affordable graphics power for games and web.

Not work, not productivity, not enhancing services for those with disabilities, not making work easier, or people smarter, but allowing massive amounts of bandwidth to display YouTube videos of a bicycling dog, baby hippos, and an unending stream of drunken karaoke singers.

# Where did this come from?

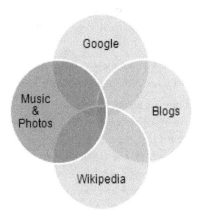

This is not all bad, and it is not all new. From my observations, tracking the industry over the past decade, it likely started with the launch of internet music download sites. They, and popular tools like Google, were probably the forerunners. They made information available for free and people flocked to these sites, beyond all expectations. Of course, advertising dollars quickly followed.

TV and newspapers also presume an inner awareness of vernacular, language and meaning that is lost on many people.

So the Web 2.0 sites and their twisted use of language, spelling and grammar are probably here to stay.

Citizen journalism is becoming common, with people on the street suddenly broadcasting breaking news on CNN. In a 60-second clip, you might hear one witness say "three men ran from the bank shooting guns," and another say "one man walked out, and no shots were fired." So is this news? Is it journalism?

On television, we're asked to text-message our vote on the best American Idol performer, rate the president's speech, and decide whether a criminal should be set free.

Blogs, Google, and Wikipedia, the online encyclopedia opened doors for people to share online. Open-source technology lets anyone do anything. What the photo and music sharing pioneers proved is that millions of people would actually spend time chasing these ideas. The Web 2.0 sites are interactive, not passive, so there are more eyeballs looking at ads, spending money on products and services advertised. Those dollars fuel even more venture capital funding for sites and spin-offs.

Even consumer magazines and newspapers are moving toward social interaction with blogs, restaurant and movie reviews, and dozens of other sites they own, geared to specific demographics, dividing their readers/subscriber into niche segments. These publications stream continuous updates to Facebook and Twitter, changing "news" from a once daily event to a non-stop flow.

We hear a great deal in the media about every fad,
including these:

> Facebook
> LinkedIn
> MySpace
> Twitter
> YouTube

But they represent just a small sampling of over 100
popular social media sites as of this writing. And
remember, worldwide, there are millions of people using
sites developed in other countries and used in other
languages than English.

Tomorrow we might wake up to a new name, and a new
millionaire investor who makes it big by creating
something people want and making it available free.

(All sites above end in .com, since they are commercial ventures).

# Meme ...a little history

Origin: Greek word used in genetics: mimeme, meaning "something imitated."

A **meme** comprises a unit of cultural information, the building block of cultural evolution or diffusion that propagates from one mind to another analogous to the way in which a gene propagates from one organism to another as a unit of genetic information and of biological evolution.

Biologist and evolutionary theorist Richard Dawkins coined the term *meme* in 1976. He gave these examples: tunes, catch-phrases, beliefs, clothing fashions, and the technology of building arches.

100 years before that, Mark Twain in *A Literary Nightmare*, describes his encounter with a jingle so "catchy" that it plays over and over in his mind until he finally sings it out loud and infects others (also known as an earworm).

# But it's not all bad

Chat groups, forums, online list-servs covering medical issues, finances, small business, parenting groups — those are all examples of social engineering. People are free to participate, share information and help others with what they learned.

Many groups share photo albums online and over 70 percent of web users reach out to Wikipedia for information and use Google as a verb.

# Social Media = Big $$$

Facebook now has broken through the 500 million user level, as of this writing. Microsoft paid $240 million for a 1.6 percent share of the social networking site in October, 2007. Not bad, considering Facebook did not even exist until 2004. Yet in an American Customer Satisfaction Index released in July 2010,. Facebook has many users who don't love the product. The Facebook approval rating was 64 points on a 100-point scale. For a popular, free service to score only 64 points prove the ephemeral nature of what's deemed an internet success today. (source: Washington Post, 7-20-10.)

"Facebook ads," is a system designed to allow advertisers to customize their marketing for specific users on the site. Some of these advertisers include heavy-hitters like major consumer electronics and media companies.

Facebook users now have greater privacy concerns than just who's looking at their pictures and profile. If advertisers are analyzing our online activity, and probing our personal profiles, the "free sharing" of information will end.

As this book went to press, Twitter announced it received $25 million in funding to make all that Twitter chatter searchable. *Business Week* reports this cash infusion will make three-year old Twitter profitable for the first time. User posts will be searchable on Google and Bing, but no word yet on how many users will object to having their casual short messages archived online for the world to see.

Mashable.com suggests Twitter may be "worth" $1.4 billion.

www.businessweek.com/technology/content/dec2009/tc20091220_549879.htm

http://mashable.com/2010/03/04/facebook-twitter-valuations/

# How many users?????

**The stats on social media users**

**Facebook:** More than 500 million active users

**Twitter:** Over 105 million registered users, 300,000 new users daily, 60% from outside U.S

**LinkedIn:** Over 70 million members in over 200 countries

Sources:
Facebook: facebook.com/press/info.php?statistics
Twitter: bit.ly/dbHgb7
LinkedIn: press.linkedin.com/about

To avoid mental overload, our primary discussion of social media covers only Facebook, LinkedIn, and Twitter, the three most popular for personal and business use.

Of course, that's just today, and it could change tomorrow. Other social media sites that you may wish to explore include:

Bebo, Digg, Friendster, iLike, LivingSocial, Myspace, Ning, Orkut, Plaxo and Second Life. YouTube could belong in this list, but to most of us, it's a one-way video channel.

Wikipedia is not strictly social media, but it does have a free, collaborative component to build libraries of training materials, documentation and project histories.

Learn much more at socialmediastatistics.wikidot.com/

# A sampling of social media sites used by adults & teens

| | |
|---|---|
| Digg, Furl, Stumbleupon Reddit.com: learn what people are clicking on. | Wikipedia, wikimedia wiktionary (collaborative websites). |
| Instant messaging and text messages result in LoudTalk and Twitter. Twitter asks "What are you doing?" | Technorati: a blog search engine. New programs search only social network sites. |
| My Space once held 85 percent of the market. Facebook was restricted to school users until Sept. 2006. Now it's larger than MySpace. | You Tube: millions of audio/video files posted by companies as well as amateurs. |
| Others: Second Life Photo sites, such as Ofoto, Flickr, Snapfish | Yap provides voice-to-text translation services for mobile phones. Users can say anything they like and Yap will send a text copy to anyone of their contacts. |

There is a large concern that what is on the web becomes vernacular made up by "a boy in his bedroom," that we have no backup for this enormous online world and it literally has no basis in reality. Yet fortunes are made, investors reap profits, and the spiral continues.

Because users can create any content, you have to make sure that what you discover is genuine. This freedom also means you can declare yourself an authority and create a Facebook page on any topic, for your favorite celebrity, charity, or book group.

When we later discuss set-up details, you'll see you can create a Facebook page that is public, or can restrict your page like a private users group.

# Children's online activities

Facebook, originally started as a way for students to keep in touch, was primarily used by teen and pre-teen children. Use was restricted only to those with a dot-edu email address, meaning school-age children, through college.

As a result of the early use among children, there was great controversy about the content, about peer-pressure, and extreme bullying.

Now that adults make up such a large percentage the age range and types of content visible to both children and adults has blended into some level of societal norms.

# Social networking:
# The effects on children

| Potential benefits | Likely Risks |
| --- | --- |
| - Reinforce friendships<br>- Expand socialization skills<br>- Make plans<br>- Private email<br>- Users surveyed:<br>-   46 percent use daily | - Cyber-bullies<br>- Danger: flirting, hidden identities, fraud, mob psychology<br>- Dumbing down of culture<br>- Illiteracy |

As an author and computer consultant, I don't learn this from kids on the street, but from Business Week, Forbes, Microsoft research labs, the Wall Street Journal, and the Macarthur Foundation which recently invested $50 million to learn more about the effects of this social networking craze.

One example of a social media site that seems to have fallen popularity is SecondLife.com, where users create a fantasy personality, buy and sell goods with fake currency, called "Linden dollars," and build an entire virtual identity with avatars. We haven't heard anything about SecondLife in many months, so it may be another form of social media that's on the way out.

Pew Internet research shows generational differences in social media users, and the particular activities they pursue.

For example, 65 percent of teens use social networking sites, compared to only 35 percent of adults.

Older users dominate in use of online resources for health information, purchasing, online banking and getting government or religious information.

Excerpted from source:
www.pewinternet.org/Infographics/Generational-differences-in-online-activities.aspx

# Making sense of it all...

> Recognize sites with contributed content and sites that aggregate popular information may not be as accurate as traditional media.

> Remember the differences between journalism and opinion.

> Use "tags" to filter out the noise.

> Ads on sites and blogs may give you an idea of who is funding the site and what audience they target.

> Learn how to start, maintain your profile, manage your privacy, and how to benefit from social media sites.

Some of the best uses of social media occur within creative arts teams, grassroots organizations, neighborhood communities, business networking, affinity groups.

# Tagging

Tags, similar to keywords, are a type of weighted text. They were intended as a way for people to organize their research. They quickly became almost cultish, worn like a badge that indicates the popularity of certain terms in online searches.

Like folklore, these tagging social experiences are defined as **Folksonomy**, defined in dictionary.com as: "a type of classification system for online content, created by an individual user who tags information with freely chosen keywords; also, the cooperation of a group of people to create such a classification system."

See http://en.wikipedia.org/wiki/Tag_cloud for a discussion on accuracy, relevance and meaning.

And is online content true? It was always suspect, but now we have to hold it to a higher standard. When "anyone" can contribute material that may or may not be accurate, we lose the journalistic filter.

Even Wikipedia, the online collaborative encyclopedia says so, about it's own material:

> It is in the nature of an ever-changing work like Wikipedia that, while some articles are of the highest quality of scholarship, others are admittedly complete rubbish. We are fully aware of this."

Source:

Ten things you may not know about Wikipedia

http://en.wikipedia.org/wiki/Wikipedia:10_things_you_did_not_know_about_Wikipedia

# Tagging

Press release tags as example of using tags to filter the subset of information you want. This sample would quickly let you focus on PR announcements related to "launches" and it tells you they don't have as much depth about "shopping sites." This helps you find what you're looking for quicker.

## Sample of a tag cloud

abuse academy analysis announces approval available bank banking becomes books business california center commercial competitive compliance conference contest cut day deal deploys direct edcomm estate firm first gold group have home how industry internet invited latest launches learning major marketing medical microsoft million mobile need new now online partner planners police present product professionals property pyratecon real receives reports rocsearch sales school series services shopping site software talk test their traffic training voip website year

A sample tag cloud from Wikipedia,
depicting frequency of
words related to the term Web 2.0

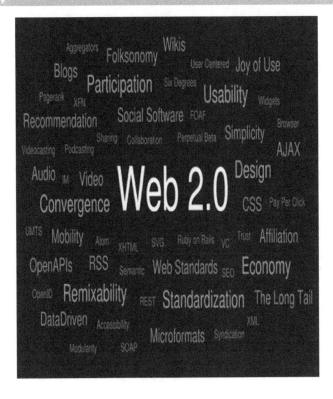

A useful tag cloud depicting world population. In the original file, each name is clickable, to drill down to further details.

Image:World Population.png

# Aggregated filters

*The New York Times measures* the amount of interest in news topics, making it easy for you to cut through the clutter and find what is most popular. Note the popularity of a topic may not be most relevant to you, but what garners the most interest among readers.

**MOST POPULAR**

E-MAILED | BLOGGED | SEARCHED

1. Age of Riches: Hedge Funds and Private Equity Alter Career Calculus

2. Do We Really Know What Makes Us Healthy?

3. Ayn Rand's Literature of Capitalism

4. Op-Ed Contributor: This Is Your (Father's) Brain on Drugs

5. Alabama Plan Brings Out Cry of Resegregation

6. The DNA Age: Cancer Free at 33, but Weighing a Mastectomy

7. Paul Krugman: Sad Alan's Lament

8. Parrot Power: Alex Wanted a Cracker, but Did He Want One?

9. Japanese Housewives Sweat in Secret as Markets Reel

10. Argentine Church Faces 'Dirty War' Past

Go to Complete List »

The New York Times

# Effects on society

A BBC News report on September 11, 2007 states an
employment law firm studied 3,500 UK companies and
projected 233 million hours are lost <u>every month</u> as a
result of employees "wasting time" on social networking.
Facebook was the prime culprit.

## Maybe we should call it
## social notworking!

The BBC report clarifies this is not a problem unique to the
United States. People the world over use these sites,
spending time and money on what sure looks like
meaningless and maybe voyeuristic behavior.

http://news.bbc.co.uk/2/hi/technology/6989100.stm

What about socialization skills? Will this delivery of random information from random sources change the way children learn and make critical judgments?

These are the questions facing our society today. Time will tell whether the implications of this consumer-generated online universe will affect education, journalism, and the national economy.

We know this much: Some Web 2.0 sites have dwindling participation as people drop out of the hype and distraction. Are they moving on to better things, or creating the next new trend? Time will tell.

# Benefits of Web 2.0

Is there any redeeming value in Web 2.0?

Of course. There's value in information sharing, having a channel of instant communication, and it is useful even in emergencies.

Additionally...

- Thousands of artists and writers are making money on Web 2.0 and may be unable to afford such visibility otherwise.

- People with disabilities can work from home and fully participate in an online environment.

- Non-profits can maintain visibility with a bigger audience at lower cost with the internet instead of traditional outreach through costly direct mail.

- Web 2.0 provides room for discussion, dialog, and broader access to media than TV & radio.

# For a more thorough evaluation of this topic, consider these books:

*Everything Is Miscellaneous: The Power of the New Digital Disorder* by David Weinberger

*The Cult of the Amateur - How Blogs, MySpace, YouTube, and the Rest of Today's User-Generated Media are Destroying Our Economy, Our Culture, and Our Values* by Andrew Keen

*The Cluetrain Manifesto: The End of Business as Usual* by Christopher Locke and Rick Levine

*The Shallows: What the Internet Is Doing to Our Brains* by Nicholas Carr.

# Ready to sign up?

## *Facebook & Twitter & LinkedIn, Oh My....*

If you want to see what all the hype is about, sign up for free accounts at Facebook.com and Twitter.com. All of the major social media sites are free of charge.

Ask a friend to invite you to join LinkedIn.com. If you offer something useful, and build a following, there's no doubt you could benefit from these sites for fun and networking.

I used to boast that *I'm a Twitter quitter* but I recently signed up for two reasons: It become harder to understand it in the abstract, and I learned many colleagues were making valuable connections. It sure won't become an addiction for me. I manage it in about four minutes a day using echofon.com to view Twitter summaries in the corner of my Firefox browser.

# About ... facebook

Facebook.com acquired over 500 million subscribers since
its launch in 2004. About 100 million are in the U.S.
Users create a page to display their interests, photos,
links to friends. They keep connected and the population
keeps growing, so exponential growth in friends,
networks, and pages seems unstoppable today.
Facebook reports over 50 percent of active users log on
in any given day.

Facebook offers tutorials and how-to guides for publishing
and sharing your material.

To get started — just sign up (see next page). You may wish
to use a secondary email address, so people who find
you on Facebook or any of the social media sites, won't
clog your main email account. Yahoo Mail and Google's
Gmail accounts have all the storage space you could
need.

# Step1. Sign up at facebook.com

# Step 2. Control your settings

Once signed in, you can create your basic profile. Return to it later if it feels overwhelming, and consider just how much info you really want to share publicly.

Beyond your profile, you can link with friends, use your Facebook inbox to keep track of people, or forward the messages to your regular email address. You use "status updates" to type notes about what you are doing, or to ask a question to your readers.

Whatever you do or say online is public. Anything on Facebook can be found by anyone, but their privacy policy states:

"Facebook created public search listings in 2007 to enable people to search for your name and see a link to your Facebook profile. They will still only see a basic set of information." Review Facebook's full privacy settings to control your Friends list, and decide which comments and photos should be kept private.

http://www.allFacebook.com/2009/02/Facebook-privacy/

Settings: Facebook is made up of many linked groups or networks, you can join them, or wait to be invited by friends who notice you're there. You can also visit the Notifications tab under Settings to determine how you want to be notified when someone wants to contact you. There are methods to remind you of birthdays, to sort and share your photos, join groups, and get invited to events.

None of this has to be done when you're first starting out. Take your time, read through other profiles, and add more when you're ready.

We already face internet privacy invasions all over the web: browsers, internet providers, sites that track the pages we visit, there's really no way to ensure your full privacy worldwide without using strong privacy tools.

Visit the Electronic Frontier Foundation (www.eff.org) for more information on how to protect your privacy. It's not just a social media issue anymore, but online purchases, tweets and text messages from phones, etc. that have the potential to track too much private information.

# About ... **Linked** in.

Let's get serious now...

One example of a potentially productive business
resource is the social media site called
linkedin.com.

Remember networking, with "Hello" badges and a
handshake? LinkedIn works in a similar way.
LinkedIn profile page displays your portfolio,
your network, and links to people you know.
They become possible connections for your
colleagues.

# Step1. Sign up at linkedin.com

Your profile at linkedin.com might be more extensive than a public Facebook page, since it connects you with business people and professional affiliations. You can choose to list your current and former employer, work history, education and connections.

Use it to recommend others you've worked with, refer people to sites of interest, invite others to join, and ask for connections.

When filling out your profile, if you include schools and former employers, you can reconnect with people you've lost track of, or who are in transition. Because you share a former employer or school, their LinkedIn home page will suggest you are a person they might wish to connect with.

The exponential growth in your LinkedIn network isn't who you know, but who they know. You might have 16 connections, but their connections can expand your visibility to hundreds or thousands of people.

## LinkedIn Groups:

LinkedIn's service is rich with affinity groups, so you can narrow your circle to those with similar interests to yours. Whether for personal or business networking, you'll have an easy time making productive relationships if you are an active participant.

There are multi-lingual groups for every profession, and every business sector.

LinkedIn was formed in 2003. Today, they have over 70 million members across the globe.

# About ... twitter™

Twitter.com has really caught on. It is a "micro-blogging" site where users keep in touch with each other by typing short messages (under 140 characters).

The constant stream of people text-messaging (texting) each other seems like a fad that will die quickly. Yet many companies are embracing it as a way to stay in front of their audience.

For quick text messages, Twitter seem to have cornered the market for now. Twitter is another free application, but your messages are limited to 140 characters of text. As a result it is referred to as "micro-blogging," with little snippets of what you're up to. For all the friends and followers who track your Twitter name, they instantly see what's going on in your world. Quick Twitter messages are called "tweets" and your tweets can automatically appear on Facebook, like status updates, so all your friends can follow you along all day. Of course, if you have 300 friends and they all tweet you all day, you probably won't get much else done.

# Sign up at twitter.com

A sample 140 -character message:

Twitter is a txt-msg service. U type up 2 140 char of text. It's ref. to as micro-blogging, cause you kn only post little snip of what U R doing right now. It kn be hard 2 read.

We learned earlier that Facebook is the size of a huge country. Now let's look at the unique language of Twitter.

Tweet – a message or comment.

Retweet (or RT) is how you forward something interesting.

Following – signing up to receive tweets from others.

Trending –An analytical snapshot showing what people are following. We're seeing this on other media sites too.

Hash tags, represented by the pound sign, index a word for search by others, such as #brownout during a widespread summer storm.  Use #cclarity to reach me.

Now what's the use of this? That's what I wondered, but in a few short years, Twitter attracts millions of fans who sure think it's cool. What becomes of grammar, spelling and punctuation? These sites could be contributing to the great dumbing-down of our culture.

The folks at Twitter say:

> "Twitter solves information overload by changing expectations traditionally associated with online communication. At Twitter, we ask one question, "What's happening?" The answers to this question are for the most part rhetorical. In other words, users do not expect a response when they send a message to Twitter."

The questions you'll soon be asking yourself:

Who has time to keep up with these sites?
Are they fads that will soon pass?

It's possible, and it's also likely that the time we spend
   cultivating these teeny corners of the web might be
   better spent elsewhere.

Twitter may be a passing fad, but if so, something else
   will take its place. An industry that supports billions of
   dollars in advertising is not without its value. Twitter is
   among the firms looking for a revenue model – a fee-
   based system that would make sense, and somehow
   add enough value for users to continue their growth.

For an in-depth understanding of how Twitter can help
   you, especially in business, visit
   business.twitter.com/twitter101/starting

# Making Twitter work for you

Ideally, your time on Twitter is either spent
   cultivating the right followers, or learning from
   what you read.
If you follow the right people, Twitter can be your
   daily go-to source for up-to-date information.
Learn by watching the etiquette of other users.
   Thank people for a mention, retweet items of
   interest, and create interesting tweets.
Not everyone you follow will prove useful. You can
   stop following people with just a click.

I heard Scott Stratten, of Un-Marketing.com at
recent conference in Chicago. His best advice is to
"Write retweetable content every single day." Just
commenting on other people's posts won't get you
very far. But write something of value, that has
impact, and it may be retweeted around the world.
He also uses brief comments, under 120 characters.
Why? It allows the retweeter to add a few words of
their own, when they circulate his comments.

# About ... You Tube™

YouTube is not exactly a social networking site, where you'd contact someone to make plans for a movie, but plays a strong role in the social, interactive aspects of the web today.

YouTube was founded in 2005, and is now owned by Google. It is the dominant video upload and sharing community online today.

YouTube combines social media with audio/video and contains millions of files, viewed daily. The ability to create and upload video directly from cell phones and webcams adds to the popular use.

You might find about 80 percent of the uploaded content to be boring, but the 20 percent with some redeeming value represents an unprecedented opportunity for free promotion for your work and your cause.

# Using YouTube

As with Facebook and other sites, YouTube has generous "Help" resources in their free online handbook:

http://www.youtube.com/t/yt_handbook_home

Beyond uploading home video, and watching video of concerts, lectures, and loads of funny stuff, like laughing babies, many people use digital cameras to shoot interesting videos, documentaries, and record music. There are bands and performers who got "discovered" by their videos on YouTube. The industry notices when a video gets thousands of clips,. If the content is really good, and the fan base is there, late-night TV can be the next step toward fame.

**YouTube reports that 20 minutes of video is uploaded <u>every minute.</u>**

As we've all learned, a talented person discovered on "American Idol" or a similar TV program can result in millions of fans almost overnight. As people log onto YouTube and download the music, recording contracts and stardom will follow within weeks, to capture the momentum of sudden celebrity.

There have been "overnight sensations" discovered as long as we've had broadcast radio or television, but now "overnight" literally means what it says. The pace of technology accelerates both good and bad media attention.

# So what's the problem with social media?

For starters, it seems to be the tipping point for further dumbing down of America. Culture is reduced to sound bites, people judge the popularity of something based on peer opinion instead of fact. We're seeing a trend toward "consumer journalism," where an eye-witness becomes an expert on national television, because they have a cell phone with a camera. That's not journalism, that's social networking.

Text messaging by typing abbreviated shorthand is not communication. Do we want a generation that can't speak in full sentences, can't form thoughts, can't think independently?

Collectively, popular social media sites are considered an amateur wasteland, and that's probably true for about 80 percent of the content created.

When we view "trending topics" on Google or national newspapers, and the topics are all celebrity or nonsense, it is cause for concern, at least to an educated populace.

Avoid sinking too much time into your online social status without considering:

× Whether it's the right place to build a presence,

× Whether other people on the sites are a good match for your goals and interests, and

× Whether you're spending too much time, or revealing too much information, without any real direction or purpose.

How much is too much?

Use Twitter for **20 minutes** , spend **5 minutes** on MySpace, **20 minutes** reading other blogs on RSS, **30 minutes** checking out photos of friends on Facebook, **20 minutes** checking out the latest threads on our favorite forums, back to Twitter for **20 minutes, 15 minutes** following links, and you might be wasting too much time.

× Source: www.problogger.net/archives/2009/05/04/plan-build-profile-readership/#more-7380

# Part Three

## Social Media --

Five ways to make it work for you:

1. Sign up
2. Control your privacy settings
3. Communication
4. Networking
5. Marketing

# Social Media Step 1
# Create an account

Whether you're interested in jumping onboard with the social media sites described in this handbook, or are ready to expand your internet use for a site where you can sell art online, join a quilting club, book group, or job search site, it's easy to get started. If you don't like it, you can always unsubscribe from a site, or just stop using it.

To get you started, most online firms require the same basic information: Your real name, a user name and a password.

With adequate anti-virus and spyware protection, you're not at great risk in normal use of the social media sites. Use the same caution in giving our private information as you do elsewhere on the web. Don't click on links that don't look legitimate, and don't "friend" people if it doesn't feel right.

You do not have to accept, or even acknowledge, every "friend" invitation you receive. Be especially cautious with children's photos and revealing details such as an upcoming vacation.

# Social Media Step 2 Privacy

When you first create an account, don't feel compelled to include all the information requested. Start out by giving only the required data, usually noted by an asterisk, for required fields.

Control your privacy settings by viewing the fine-print before you finish the sign-up process. While you can change your preferences later, some information, once made public, is difficult to retract.

Most online firms have statements like this, and its up to you to read them.

"Review our Privacy Policies to learn more about the kind of data that is collected about you, with whom it is shared, and for what purposes."

# Social Media Step 3 Communication

Just as we don't want to forward email jokes to people, we don't want to get stuck on sites that are a waste of time, and lead to loads of other people asking to become our friend. Sometimes we need to escape from the chatter of the world, and these sites can drain both our time and mental clarity.

For most of us, this would seem overwhelming, but if you like technology and you're at the computer, cell phone, iPhone, or Blackberry where you can keep up with the messages and reply, it's a fun way to keep in touch. In fact, it may be cutting down on email overload, since you keep up with these social networking sites on the go.

Perhaps that's better than sitting down at your computer at 9 p.m. and finding you have to spend an hour weaving through threads of email you missed while you were away from the computer.

How to manage your time:

If you visit your Facebook or LinkedIn page daily, you'll see an inbox with messages from friends. You can also set "Status updates" so you can keep people informed of what you're doing, and receive their updates.

Have comments emailed to you, if you don't want to have to check each site.

And, rather than have an all-consuming involvement in social media sites, remember the focus is communication. If someone wants to contact you on a particular topic, they are more likely do so by email or phone, not by leaving a public message.

# Social Media Step 4 Networking

Consider the social aspect of 'social media' and use your relationships to network. Networking has always been a powerful tool for business development and for putting people together for mutual benefit.

> Examples: Provide job leads, offer suggestions for time-saving strategies, share ideas, introduce your friends to each other.

On Facebook, you could do this by sending a status update or message.

On LinkedIn, you could invite someone into your network.

An effective technique is to cross-promote on each of these sites.

> Examples: before writing a blog post, send a Twitter message on the topic to gauge interest. When posted, put it on Facebook, and LinkedIn.

> At LinkedIn start a discussion and refer back to the blog post. Or ask a question seeking an expert opinion on non-profits, and you'll probably receive targeting information.

Remember your LinkedIn page might be seen by professional colleagues and affiliate organizations, while your Facebook page might be viewed by your former spouse, your in-laws, or your boss.

This is one reason to remember that everything you post online is public. You might make a comment in a Facebook discussion about "the client who's driving you nuts..." only to have that client read your page later, and get the sense that you're talking about him.

It's best to maintain a professional tone in your public posts, and create another site or identity for personal purposes. We've often read of a coach or teacher who lost their job because of photos posted online showing them drinking or caught on-camera goofing around at a party. The worldwide web is truly that, and, for better or worse, its also nearly instant feedback in our lives today.

# Social Media Step 5 Marketing

If I had to define the difference between networking and marketing, I'd say:

Networking is widening your circle to reach the most relevant and influential people you can.

Marketing is shining a light on the specific things you do.

Use your contact network to gain business or to promote interest in your organization or group. Instead of heavy-hitting promotion, though, try to provide value for people who are taking the time to read your comments.

Some ideas:

- Offer new information
- Write a helpful article
- Post photos of your products or events
- Suggest five ways to benefit from what you offer
- Highlight the value of volunteering, supporting the local community.

To cultivate relationships and keep readers interested in your social media sites, you can't neglect them.

So, of course, there's an app for that… You can use a service such as ping.fm, hootsuite.com,. To dig deeper, use sphinn.com, an internet marketing discussion forum.

If your relationships are distinctly different on LinkedIn compared to personal posts on Facebook and Twitter, don't automatically link all the sites.

Remember, you don't want to waste your reader's time with irrelevant information, especially on LinkedIn.

# The scope of social media in 2010

Twitter analysts estimate that there are 1.2 million active
users, posting more than 2.25 million tweets every day.,
including this gem:

http://www.huliq.com/3257/78826/aniston-dumps-mayer-
over-twitter-obsession-report

So, is there anything worthwhile on Twitter? Sure.
Especially large companies and non-profits who got on
board early on. They have learned to send sound-bites
out all day, promoting their work or their causes.

Political activism, news sites, and groups such as
NatureConservancy.org are examples you might wish
to check out. You'll see a banner like this on most large
web sites:

Join The Nature Conservancy on

 flickr

Facebook          Flickr          Twitter

# Facebook in perspective

"If Facebook were a country, it would be the eighth most
   populated in the world, just ahead of Japan, Russia
   and Nigeria."

   Mark Zuckerberg, Facebook co-founder 1/09


While originally a cool tool for teens, Facebook now,
   according to a Hitwise.com report, shows that the
   average age of the Facebook user has gone up.
   Adults between 25 and 44 years old now make up
   more than half of the social network's user base, up
   from just 32 percent a year ago.


If teens are backing off because Facebook has lost its
   cool, advertisers will either change to appeal to older
   users, or the site may experience further decline.

# The state of social media

Astonishing growth rates in social media are
compounded exponentially by users pulling in all
their friends, expanding the synergies between
and among the sites,.

For example: you could use LinkedIn, sending updates
to Facebook, then let people know by sending a
tweet via Twitter and retweet with status updates
all day.

Or use one site, such as FriendFeed to keep track of
what your friends are doing online.

Twitter soared into popularity but, as of this writing, may have reached a peak. A possible decline is indicated by recent stories in the media saying Twitter is flat-lining, and growth has slowed.

Since social media sites all compete for our time, and all can do the same thing: (stay in touch, share music and photos), we may soon see greater convergence.

It seems there is no limit to the capacity of the internet, or of people willing to spend time populating millions of pages with transitory information.

It's doubtful that the volume of services that comprise the existing social media sites will all remain. Until they sort themselves out, though, we will continue to see more innovations, such as a "Flickr2Twitter" service, to share your Flickr photos on Twitter.

# Computing chaos?

**Remember where the tech industry started:**

> **A desire for a computer in every home in America**
> **Affordable internet access across the country**
> **An earnest goal to bridge the digital divide.**

Enormous research, funding, and resources were used to create the internet, and make high-speed access available around the world.

Then came the flood of information, too much to absorb, leaving us to parse all the data available, and focus on what has meaning for each of us.

It should all come down to something more than chaotic chatter. This technology is likely to improve, so we can expect broader choices, linking us to important cultural trends. The future will be one in which we can stay informed, aware, and tuned in, to whatever extent we desire.

# It's up to you

Just as the social experience varies from person to
person – some like rock concerts, others hip-hop. A
second group might be private and reclusive.

The third group wants to participate to know what is
going on but not become a slave to technology.

A fourth group feels they've got to be there. They were
first to have a WII computer game console, started
tweeting on Twitter while getting a haircut, and
uploading a photo to Facebook so friends could vote
on the new haircut.

Just as some people look forward to opera, and others
turn off the radio at the first aria, so too, social
networking is not for everyone.

If you're on all the social media sites, and able to
upload video from your cell phone to YouTube,
you're a social media star. It's all out there, and for
now, it's all free, thanks to advertisers eager to be
seen by millions daily. So embrace it. You're part of
the "It" generation.

The rest of us are right behind you, waiting to see what
happens next.

## BLOG POWER AND SOCIAL MEDIA HANDBOOK CHART

# Your Six-Week Plan

Week 1: Blog – read a few good ones, then start yours and list your blog in directories. On your blog, build your blogroll of other favorite blogs.

Week 2: Create a profile on Facebook and Twitter, or add your blog link if already have an existing profile. Create a LinkedIn profile to expand your professional network. If you're lazy, link all your social media sites to update at the same time

Link to people of interest, keep your profile current, with status updates

Week 3 It's time to update your blog. You should add content, ask a question, or quote something interesting at least once a week; twice is better.

Week 4: Revisit your social media pages, and add a status update or join a relevant group to begin hearing from people who share your interests.

Week 5: Monetize. Yes, there are ways to make money with your social media presence. Besides getting paid to write for other blogs, you can earn ad revenue. Visit Google.com/adsense to learn how, and zenhabits.com to learn how Leo Babuta makes so much money with his blog.

Week 6: Keep going, if you enjoy the social nature of Web 2.0 and if it is working for you. Fit these tools into your weekly time at the computer, at your own pace. It should take less than an hour a week to view, update, and reply to others with relevant and credible comments.

# I CAN DO THIS....

**BLOG NAME IDEAS**

| | |
|---|---|
| | |
| | |
| | |
| | |

**PHOTOS**

| | |
|---|---|
| | |
| | |
| | |
| | |

**START AN EMAIL LIST**

| | |
|---|---|
| | |
| | |
| | |
| | |

**SCHEDULE**

| | | |
|---|---|---|
| | DATE: | BLOG POST 1 |
| | DATE: | BLOG POST 2 |
| | DATE: | BLOG POST 3 |
| | DATE: | BLOG POST 4 |

**FUTURE IDEAS**

| | |
|---|---|
| | |
| | |
| | |

# For each social media service, start with two things in mind:

1. Your goals
2. Your intended audience

Then consider your core focus. Does it fit your goals and will it be of interest to your readers?

What role do you want to play: create discussion, be seen as an expert, get speaking gigs?

How will each social media element help you accomplish this? If one is not useful, don't waste time with it.

Evaluate your six-week plan. Comment on other people's posts, create at least one new item, check your traffic. Is it doing what you want? Are you adding traffic and building a network to share your interests?

# Blog Resources

Blogcatalog.com
Blogger.com
Cclarity.com/blogbookcando.pdf
Cclarity.com/blogbookcando.doc
Gallagherink.com/webblog.html
Problogger.com
Technorati.com
Thebestofblogs.com
Typepad.com
Wordpress.com


# Social Media Resources
Echofon.com
Eff.org
Hitwise.com
Lifehacker.com
PewInternet.org
SocialMediaToday.com

# Notes

# Notes

# Notes

# Notes

# Notes

# Notes

# Notes

# Notes

# Notes

# Notes

# Notes

# Notes

# Notes

# Notes

# Notes

# Notes

# Notes

**Author**

Helen Gallagher is national speaker and consultant on publishing and technology. A full presentation on the risks/benefits of using social media sites is available for presentation to your group.

Other books by the author:

*Computer Ease*

*Release Your Writing:*
*Book Publishing Your Way*

Helen's business, Computer Clarity, is celebrating over a decade of consulting success with clients around the U.S. More information is available at www.releaseyourwriting.com.

Contact Helen@cclarity.com

www.ingramcontent.com/pod-product-compliance
Lightning Source LLC
LaVergne TN
LVHW052301060326
832902LV00021B/3651